SOME
SAY
THE
LARK

11 10 9 8 7 6 5 4 3 2

Alice James Books are published by Alice James Poetry Cooperative, Inc., an affiliate
of the University of Maine at Farmington.

Alice James Books
114 Prescott Street
Farmington, ME 04938
www.alicejamesbooks.org

Library of Congress Cataloging-in-Publication Data
Names: Chang, Jennifer, 1976- author.
Title: Some say the lark / Jennifer Chang.
Description: Farmington, ME : Alice James Books, 2017.
Identifiers: LCCN 2017021877 (print) | LCCN 2017025047 (ebook) | ISBN
    9781938584718 (eBook) | ISBN 9781938584664 (paperback)
Subjects: | BISAC: POETRY / American / General.
Classification: LCC PS3603.H3573 (ebook) | LCC PS3603.H3573 A6 2017 (print) |
    DDC 811/.6--dc23
LC record available at https://lccn.loc.gov/2017021877

 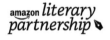

Cover design by Anna Reich
annareichdesign.com

SOME
SAY
THE
LARK

POEMS

JENNIFER CHANG

CONTENTS

ACKNOWLEDGMENTS

Grateful acknowledgment is due to the following publications and their editors, where some of these poems first appeared, sometimes with different titles and in different forms: *American Poetry Review, The PBS NewsHour's Art Beat, A Public Space, At Length, Blackbird, Boston Review, Kenyon Review, Kenyon Review Online, Narrative, The Nation, New England Review, The New Yorker, Orion, Poetry, Poetry Northwest, The Rumpus, Salt Hill,* and *Web Conjunctions.*

"Again a Solstice," "Freedom in Ohio," and "Patsy Cline" first appeared in the Poem-a-Day series from the Academy of American Poets.

"Dorothy Wordsworth" was republished in *Best American Poetry 2012,* edited by Mark Doty, and as Split This Rock's Poem of the Week on October 10, 2014.

"A Horse Named Never" was republished in *Monticello in Mind: Fifty Contemporary Poems on Jefferson,* edited by Lisa Russ Spaar.

      *   *   *

I owe a lifetime of gratitude to The MacDowell Colony and Yaddo for giving me and my work such generous sanctuary over the years, especially the many spent writing this book. I'm grateful to Bowling Green State University for introducing me to new landscapes, new perspectives, and new friends. Had George Washington University not given me an academic home, I would never have found my way to an end, and I am indebted to the English Department at GW and all my brilliant, good-humored colleagues on the sixth floor of Phillips Hall. Thank you to the friends who read poems or simply joined me in picking apart the art and language of everyday life: Lindsay Bernal, Gaby Calvocoressi, Amber Dermont, David Francis, Sarah Gambito, Jenny Kronovet, Joseph Legaspi, Aimee Nezhukumatathil, Justin Quarry, Angeline Shaka, Nida Sophasarun, and the Spaarlings. I would be remiss if I did not thank Elizabeth Fowler and Jahan Ramazani, who have taught me more about the valley of each poem's saying than they'll ever know. For keeping me somewhat sane, idiosyncratically loved, and always well-fed, I thank my family, the Changs, and to the youngest of this family, the Rhodes-Chang boys, I'm grateful for how stunningly they changed the course of everything, this book included. I am in awe of Carey Salerno, Alyssa Neptune, Erica Wright, and the staff of Alice James Books, who have my every gratitude for the joyful tenacity with which they bring books to life.

And for reading so often and, best of all, so well, I thank my fellow pilgrim souls, Jenny Johnson and Cecily Parks.

This book is for my husband, who once told me I was ferocious and then let me be fool enough to believe him. I thank him for that, the life we share, and so much more.

FOR EVAN

I was alone, till some involuntary sympathetic emotion, like the attraction of adhesion, made me feel that I was still a part of a mighty whole, from which I could not sever myself—.... Futurity, what hast thou not to give to those who know that there is such a thing as happiness!

—Mary Wollstonecraft, *Letters Written during a Short Residence in Sweden, Norway, and Denmark*

Juliet. Wilt thou be gone? It is not yet near day.
It was the nightingale, and not the lark,
That pierced the fearful hollow of thine ear.
Nightly she sings on yond pomegranate tree.
Believe me, love, it was the nightingale.

—William Shakespeare, *Romeo and Juliet*, Act III, Scene V

A HORSE NAMED NEVER

At the stables, each stall was labeled with a name.

Biscuit stood aloof—I faced always, invariably, his clockwork tail.

Crab knew the salt lick too well.

Trapezoid mastered stillness: a midnight mare, she was sternest and tallest, her chest stretched against the edges of her stall.

I was not afraid of Never, the chestnut gelding, so rode his iron haunches as far as Panther Gap.

Never and I lived in Virginia then.

We could neither flee nor be kept.

Seldom did I reach the little mountain without him, the easy crests making valleys of indifferent grasses.

What was that low sound I heard, alone with Never?

A lone horse, a lodestar, a habit of fear.

We think of a horse less as the history of one man and his sorrows than as the history of a whole evil time.

I fed him odd lettuce, abundant bitterness.

Who wore the bit and harness, who was the ready steed.

Or: *I think there be six Nevers in the field.*

He took the carrot, words by my own reckoning, an account of creeks and oyster catchers.

I named my account "Notes on the State of Virginia."

It was bred for show and not to race.

Never, I cried, *Never*.

Were I more horse than rider, I would better understand the beast I am.

Our hoof-house rested at the foot of the mountain, on which rested another house more brazen than statuary.

Let it be known: I first mistook gelding for gilding.

I am the fool that has faith in Never.

Somewhere, a gold door burdened with apology refuses all mint from the yard.

THE WINTER'S WIFE

It will be years before I understand
failure. The sun's last rage
in the winter trees. My yard
is a failure of field. It is small
and poorly tended. Years before
this hard kernel of worry
rises to a truer height, I can learn
to make shade with my palms,
but I cannot learn to unmoor my want.
I want wild roots to prosper
an invention of blooms, each unknown
to every wise gardener. If I could be
a color. If I could be a question
of tender regard. I know crabgrass
and thistle. I know one algorithm:
it has nothing to do with repetition
or rhythm. It is the route from number
to number (less to more, more
to less), a map drawn by proof,
not faith. Unlike twilight, I do not
conclude with darkness. I conclude.

THERE ARE TOO MANY OTHER BIRDS TO WRITE ABOUT

*at the grave of Edith Lewis, longtime
companion to Willa Cather*

Loyal stone,
I never knew you. In the city, I was a Nebraska.
I also had an ending. I swept the sky
one lousy hurt after another, dying to become
a newer field. My guts vast, impossible.
This is not autobiography. I have no memories.
I found you sleeping past the twentieth century,
where desire begins at curiosity and the balladeers
are kiting checks for unwritten songs. *O, America,*
you once sang, *why?* You trained it from New York
to Santa Fe, your love never quite measuring 3,000 miles,
and that's marriage, and that's death. *O,* America.
I'll never go far enough—wanting one man, then
another, believing every state bird
is the cardinal. For the cardinals wake me every morning
with one stuttering admonition: *she! she! she!* I'll never
shut them up. I'll never fail like a genius.
I'll open the window and howl my No,
the weakest of thunders.
A small stone marks the life of a sorrowful woman.
Are we not all her keepers? In Nebraska, I chased
a brown bird, so quiet I never learned her name.

SMALL PHILOSOPHIES

Phenomenology

Now the feverroot,
the marsh weed, the marigold.

Now the twin hours
of peony and delphinium.

Forge the clover-fraught
field, the field-fraught clover.

Permit the forest armature,
neither elm-brigade

nor garden-lust. You are a twilight
and a twilight bird. Isn't that

a sparrow
forlorn in the greenest branches?

Why forlorn? Because
the clouds have gone brute.

You are a quality
and a thing silenced

by pine-shrug. Stern willow.
Now run and hide in the fern.

Logic

The spectacular math of the walker is specular.
Sidestepping the poison oak, the walker measures
aslant. He values the verity of decency and will not
disturb New Hampshire's granite ascent.

And there is a calculus to crossing the field,
by which the walker demonstrates an unknown number
of wilting flowers. Who can grasp a lily of the valley
of the field? Every tall grass feigns wheat, and yet

and yet, rash and burn! When will the walker play
lover? When will his walk be well-companioned
and amorous? The walker's rule is recognition,
not sex. Again he seeks the fire pond of his youth.

Epistemology

Here is an icehouse that no longer houses ice.
Here is an alfalfa meadow in need of mowing.
Here is the barn where a sauced and saucy welder
has left behind his anvil. It was never his barn.
Here is a clearing in the woods that didn't exist
until December's ice storm. It was once a grove
of maiden ferns and hardwood trees. A kind man
cleared the roots and trunks, then kindly retreated.

I have stood in this clearing and cannot decide
if I miss the trees or if I love newborn clarity.
How can I love a damaged place? But I love
rooms and cities I'll never return to, and once
I loved a man for how he damaged me. Here
is the footbridge unbridged by that storm. Here
is the fire pond the walker could not find: he did not
know my route. Here is the water. Where is the fire?

WHOSO LIST TO HUNT

1

When there was such a thing as correspondence, landscape was a verb, honor was a verb.

2

I wrote on a bus and saw the city park where a king once hunted deer.

3

Yes, I wrote, *in a net I seek to hold the wind.*

4

I live in history.

5

My wild English a yellow blur of faces, a stranger's watercolors drying paper to brittleness.

6

Now my life consists of pronouns.

7

Where deer fringe the field, I stand with my hands out, another animal wanting to be free again.

8

There is a word for this, like a cobblestone dislodged from the thoroughfare.

9

Brittle page, history, what am I to you?

10

Thinking is today's minor captivity.

11

From which I won't be rescued, this delicate trespass.

12

What is nature?

13

14

Fainting I follow. I leave off therefore,

TERRA INCOGNITA

1

I know meager words to redress sorrow:
consolation and *in media res*. It is, I explain,
what sorrow needs, how it happens. A door
falls out of the frame, and you're more

open than you'd like. Tonight I was dockside,
hating you, hating, but what good is that.
My ship did not wreck, nor round a graver coast.
I sailed only so far as to always see shore.

2

Mostly I stayed home, attendant to a weight
I still can't name. I watched the waves and each
became my love: a whiplash of salt, cold constant
chorus, my heart's oceanic erudition. Because

I have never known all that feeling knows,
the sea wins the rocking contest every night,
my ship sailing without me. Of houses, I know
I am fear's familiar. You ate from my silent

plate, drank my silent imposition. Again, the sky,
in flames, begs for more—wasted clock, unread
books. There is no meaning in things or words.
More, you said. More, cried the sea. More.

3

Once, I wandered a shoreless country, its flaxen
fields vast as maps, where strangers swarmed
the streets like pollen and claimed primitive awe.
You were not there. You did not see the craft

with which I got lost. Of the world's unforgiving
order, I am grateful that it is without wrath. Our
ancient tree, struck by storm, splintered at roadside.
Please note: its destruction spared the house.

RIVER PILGRIMS

I'm the one who's raw.
I'm the one learning the river's silt
and scum, how the sediment floats
but the muck and mire

sink. Sister Elizabeth, what
did the asphalt confess?
The yellow fumes, the pink fumes,
the squat white tanks hoarding
alien fuel: my exhausted
portents! I'm the pom-pom girl
of the current apocalypse, half-
gone, all-gone, carcinogenic cloud.

The loons, grease-slick in the Hackensack,
go red-eyed with loon cries.

———

Sister Elizabeth, who will dry your dewy brow?

Winter never started and the chorus girls, the chorus girls,
are jubilant pears.
                          Can you do the cancan, the sleight
of hand, the slightly out-of-date grandstand? God's in
the soccer field. He's in your messenger bag
deleting your stump speech. Like the rain, he's all

nevermind. I have two Bartlett pears and a Chinese umbrella.

Let's go.

———

I loved my errors senseless
and was not sisterly. Do you forgive?

I don't. Look what concrete makes:
A beige cake. A mold-resistant gutter.

And still the stranger drowned.

If we follow his body,
we'll discover how the river ends:

I wager blue resolution, not the ocean,
but the ocean's childless oracle,

where the city barges congregate
and dispose of the city's waste.

The ducks have grown accustomed
to the stream of gasoline that braids itself

into each ripple. I watch their brave swimming
make white foam, sinuous ribbons

of water. How the river ends, only the ducks
and detritus will know: some fog caught

his body's midnight mission to skip
over the current like a palm-flat stone.

Now is when you explain that sorrow's
aboriginal. And platonic. Your order,

Sister Elizabeth, waves their black habits at us.
What have I told you about not waving back?

———

Sedge glistens along the turnpike.
Someone once told me the name of those flowers.
A man I wanted nothing to do with.
Another asked, *Why do women need to be girlfriends?*
We are approaching the swamp.

Too many sycamores mean not enough water.
So we grow wary of swamp dwellers.
Sexless in their low-eyed ways.
What's with the inaccessibility of leopard frogs?
Or the way Sister Elizabeth hikes up her skirt.

Joyful with dirt.
Up close I see the petals are in fact yellow.
Still another would not approve of such details.
Though I loved him.
I'd tuck honeysuckle into his wallet.

He'd point out stagnant water, that stench.
Of rotting wood and insect death.
Devotion's odd jewel: a trail without.
Shade the aloof August light joyful with dirt.
Sister Elizabeth calls memory a window.

Into new life.
I quote *Bah humbug* god of old.
Books knee-jerk god girlfriend's god.
Nor is the mud benevolent.
We stand and drown stand and drown.

———

Hackensack. Passaic. Raritan. Delaware.
New Jersey's algae, drift, and drear

clutter our map with riparian veins.
Sister Elizabeth's brandishing her ivory cane!

Today the sky glows aquamarine, tomorrow

it rains turpentine. Yes, the good smell
of the garden state, the cracked snail shells

baking on an off-white shore. Is this where
the river ends? Holy humidity,
                              can nuns wear shorts?

Your dance card, Sister Elizabeth,
lists my name beside a big, fat X. I won't ask

about the overlooked waltz or your swingtime propensities
for we are out of time:
                              downstream we cannot find his body,
                              upstream we cannot find his body.

The sum of hours equals.
I wear decay as a necklace
to spook myself. A twig in your pocket, Sister Elizabeth,

or a compass? (We are out of time.) Better question:
oak or South?

—————

Sister Elizabeth prays at the bridge.

What if.

God of steel girders. God of pigeon shit.
A feast of light
                    crumbling at our feet.

I'd rather not reach the end
only to discover
                    the end is whim,

as when that swarm of dark water
turned out to be
                    an upsetting of the river floor,

                              some wild foot
kicking out the bottom-feeders.
That clot and that inkblot.

Where is your body, Sister Elizabeth,

under the holy folds, the heat
that makes nonsense of your dress?
The bridge opens up

for us: we know
                    we will fail
                    and the current will

unlearn us, my water-skin, the ocean's clock:

we love loss as we love ourselves,
secretly. And too much.

FREEDOM IN OHIO

on my birthday

I want a future
making hammocks
out of figs and accidents.
Or a future quieter
than snow. The leopards
stake out the backyard
and will flee at noon.
My terror is not secret,
but necessary,
as the wild must be,
as sandhill cranes must
thread the meadow
yet again. Thus, autumn
cautions the cold
and the wild never want
to be wild. So what
to do about the thrum
of my thinking, the dangerous
pawing at the door?
Yesterday has no harmony
with today. I bought
a wool blanket, now shredded
in the yard. I abided by
dwelling, thought nothing
of now. And now?
I'm leopard and crane,
all's fled.

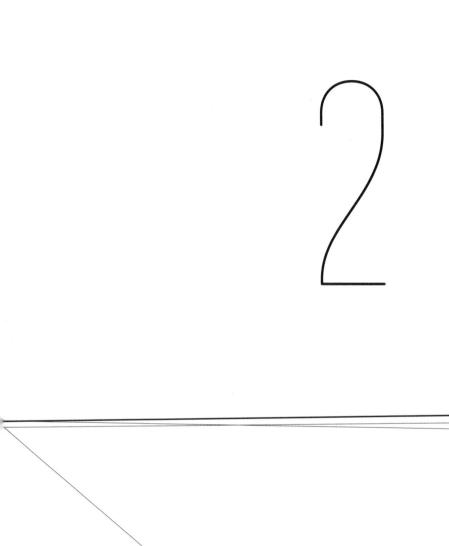

2

PATSY CLINE

She's in the desert
releasing the ashes of her father,
the ashes of her child,
or the ashes of the world. She is not

what she observes. The rare spinystar.
It does not belong to her. Bright needle threading
a cloud through the sky. There's sun enough,
there's afterlife. Her own body, a pillar of ash.
I fall to pieces, she says. Faithless

nimbus, faithless thought. In my life,
I have lost two men. One by death,
inevitable. One

by error: a waste. He wept
from a northern state,
hunger too cold
for human knowledge.

Once I was a woman with nothing to say.

Never did I say, *Ash to ash*.
Never has the desert woken me up.
I said,
Who releases whom?

Inevitably, all have known
what the desert knows. No one
will count the lupine when I'm gone.

No one looks to the sun
for meaning. For meat
I've done so much less.

Cattle in the far basin, sagebrush, sage.

I live in the city where I loved that man.
The ash of him, the self's argument.

Now and then, I think of his weeping,
how my body betrays me:
I am not done with releasing.

MYSELF—BE NOON
TO HIM

He left
my plight
wild and still

as lyric. Moths
in the sea
plume. A freak

of lightning,
no storm. The tides
cannot decide:

to evade
the shore
or crest?

If impatience. If
orbital motion.
Master it.

———

So? So? the sea asks.

I envy the one-word lexicon,

the sea's singular mastery.
So!—to declare certitude.

So?—to not care.

And so much to not care about!

Description, namely,
every word testing

what's real
only to fail.

Today I feel sad.

But somehow

this is wrong.
Gulls disappear

into the palest sky.
I feel quiet.
I am not quite myself today.

Gray wings and gray clouds.
Godwit birds outrun the tide.

Today I am a fragment of shell
thinking of him. *So?*

Yellow beach grass struck by surf.

———

Meaning is the wing
but I did not mean
so much as meander.

The black hurt
gnawing at.

The black hurt he deemed shame.

And where should I go
now that I've reached the sea?

———

I was thinking about a time
before war,

when the sea was not a border
and we dove

into the punishing
waves. Some shore noises

I forget: the hour shifting

with the tide-turn
like an octave drop, sand-scatter

against our bodies, phantom cries
from phantom children.

No more birds trace the coast,

no anxious clock, no song

other than…. Midday
amnesty. Fragment
of sun. I think

this is not the same beach.
Too thin a shoreline,

too close to town.

HOW TO LIVE IN AN AMERICAN TOWN

I woke early to find the dog once again
sleeping alone in the front room.
He dreams what I dream: blue-eyed

children somehow mine, somehow
upright as the summer grass, taller than this rain.
I have never had a dream come true.

No, not true.
There was the one about you,

the one where the kitchen catches fire,
and you are the only one who knows
not to pour water on the flame.

And the fire was like my dream children.
And everyone is standing quite tall,

our heads brushing against a low
cumulus cloud, submitting ourselves

to the blind craft of terror.
I've been unkind to strangers,

unkind to you.
I did not thank you about the fire,
which to this day still scorches.

This is true.
I opened the door and bargained

with the dog: *If you run,*
I'll relinquish the dream to you. You love the field, the blue eyes...

What do I love?
I love the dog. I love an empty room.
I want to love more than I know.

I'd like to never know the dog
dying, that he will die,
that I don't know that I don't know

he's dead now
because I'm listening to the rain.
So run with him. Please.

Take the kitchen fire.
Run, heart, run, you'll hear me

crying at the threshold.
Run as far as Duluth. Helena.
Lone Pine, California.

Run farther.

To a town like this one,
but without all the lousy rain.
I hear grief burns faster there.

HABIT

We are coldest at noon

O. is really suffering
and I do not believe
that she is suffering
fog ruins the moth
how could O. suffer
she is the song in my
mouth that won't
escape another secret
that if told would scar
I do not believe I suffer
to hold a word in my
throat until I choke a
virus or a waning pause
every few days a winter
fly slow flutter along
the wall where it hides

After the solstice, I write C.

I do not remember today
my mouth sour taste
when I woke a dream of
pickled limes I swam along
a country larger than NJ
I knew a coastal bird there

Thawing from the ice-eaves

a day of rain the walker
paused under oak cover
but the tree bare did not
protect him not a walker
I've seen before but these
are not my woods I opened
the window after lunch a

warm rain we are one week
into thaw and far from
spring foolish walker rain
hanging on branches no
form free of other forms
free of I sentence my
self in storm too early to
bed too cold the kettle

Birch or fog, I'm colder

letter from C. she reaches
Green Mountain and it is
a behemoth of ice I ask
glacier to no answer she
received my letter a week
late slow post slowpoke
O. says of all outdoor
labor winter every day
we watch weather unmake
the new stream remains
of a blizzard narrow ditch
C. would call tributary her
mother would say brook
no creek yes a kinder name

Upon sighting the walker, I note

or we watch weather make
land ice on the road too
thick to melt yet traps a
season's worth of brown
elm leaves we cannot step
an inch without looking
down each spread flat as
paper a trick on display
sun at 4 p.m. I write C.
false signals the weather
O. in cellar whistling

I marked the table with a name

patience I cannot recall
tea cold before the cake
sliced and plated patience

How we worry the letter, but say

about suffering O. will not
cease suffering F. left a
chair behind with
wobbly legs his infidelity
but O. I say what can one
expect of old furniture no
word from C. or thank god
F. but O. does not love
silence so suffers its weight
on her heart our house is
made of fog by midnight
can I let it in the parlor I
ask O. I ask can we awake
open the window the balm
outside the wrens my heart
will you not cease awake

O. asks if winter wanes

frost at dawn last week's
rain collected in the roof
gutter heavy eaves one
dollop became ice as it
dropped I believe at the
foot of yew we mistook
at first for crocus bud a
pale cotyledon no stem

Again, the question of the chair

web cornering the ceiling
vacant I hardly have words
for O. the old suffering a
habit of season C. writes
of the northern barometer
degrees she cannot chart
a line gone far I note the
wisp script what high branch
in a slow wind still there's
the fly we are less we wool-
gather as F. or some walker
once said muddy hems
these are not our woods
but we wear this fabric our
fog I walk the parlor den
O. sleeps our cold kitchen
today I found a root a name
I knew but couldn't say

THE MIDDLE AGES

Nothing is right and nothing is wrong,
my neighbor admits. She's smoking
Winstons on her stoop. I point

to the 2 p.m. cardinal
who's made a habit of our telephone wires.
My neighbor yawns

out a cloud. How does one
get over a hurt? Red bird swaying
on a fiber optic swing, red bird hapless

and no doubt male. A clock
of my wonder, the cardinal escaping.
I am holding onto the root of an unknown

plant. Not even winter explains
why cold precipitates despair or why
the parks department razing an acre of oaks

reminds me that pastoral fails yet again.
A hurt is as senseless, rising
from decay, this sequence

of trees. I'm out of season,
headless, and wormy with a forest
seizing my sad-sack gut, the cloud-

crowded sky performing a future
I refuse to claim. Smoke or sorrow,
flame or rage, this change

of landscape cannot be another
radiant loss. A yellow cat naps
in the window while at the curb

a girl twirls through wintering
azaleas and sings,
Olga, my Olga. I have no one

to forgive but myself, living here
where the past meets me
at dusk: the echo of an Olga,

my Olga, for example, who once stole
my longtime chum by being better
at jumping rope. That's one

old woe, the tiniest plaint,
that like a minute or two of bad traffic
measures a road

that might go nowhere or, better,
marks time, for once, as
immeasurable, never to end.

ON EMOTION

It was inside, gathering heat in her blood, slowly killing her.

No one said a word.

And this grew her fury further, grieved her immeasurably.

What did it look like.

A knot, or a slag of granite.

I imagined another brother, unborn for he was only a knot.

How my granite brother would never leave her.

I grew up in her abject sadness, which soon became our speaking.

And then I left.

Smaller, smaller, he was her favorite.

Jays nag the first light.

And now I am awake before dawn hoping today is a day when I won't
have to say anything.

And then I.

To me, it was unintelligible.

I could see through her skin, see my brother not growing inside her.

Would he ever come outside.

The raging jays, the squawking catastrophe.

I wanted to know.

What is the difference between a son and a daughter, I wanted to know.

That is private.

That was her answer.

EPISTEME 12

two radish leaves tell me spring has come

I sat in the nightfield
to better articulate
the stars I pretended to hate the stars

now rain
reading me well

pine quills on the western path

the hemlock clarity
of the grove the first

radishes of the season
distant traffic

outpacing my thoughts
I have one thought

noise-wrecked
a Socratic question
why jack-in-the-pulpit

in the tyranny of ailanthus trees

I bite the bitter root
of love

I unstitch rain
from waxflowers
monkshoods if loving were

the august truth
white rage hard flesh the skylark

is more hardy than the nightingale

IT WAS YOUR BIRTHDAY AGAIN

When I was a child,
we lay in the grass and the clouds
made sense to me. That's who I'll be,

I said to my friend. Later,
she'd suffer from sorrow,
a disease of mountain air, though

she loved the corner she hid in.
We never swam in the sea
is the way I now distinguish

the people who've known me long
but not very well. She knit a veil
for herself, walked under it,

and then we never swam in the sea.
I watched her once unhook dead branches
from a living tree. Her face, a sample

of summer grass. These days, I'm living
by a graveyard again. I have a new friend
with the same grand name. Farewell,

we say to the past even as our voices
tell me that speaking is religion. Fare
well, and we reignite the dead

languages, singing Latin to the sea.
Therefore, what is the graveyard
if not a sequence of recanting waves?

The names I never knew I now know
as words on stone, the kinds of prayers
that can't help themselves. I didn't go

to her wedding, and then she died.
I forgave her. Or I didn't. I cried out
her name to my new friend,

sadly: *Hello!*
Now that you've come back
what shall we do today?

MOUNT PLEASANT

All night, six vagrants stood at our stoop
chewing the fat out of a too-stout story.
She did this, did that, took that, she never,
*never, never, never, never,…*a white fluttering, a
thought, like headlights from a passing car,
lights up this room

                      where I've never been restful,
never still. Outside, the buses must be un-routing.
I hear their slowgoing screech round the corner,
engines dying. My neighbor's a dinosaur, Bonnie,
she's lived here since the commune days,
eats hempseed, I bet, always nods at me. It's not her
out there, but she's in my head, the lonely field
I imagine each night, awake again
nowhere else to go.

                  Never is
a strange design, to name what can't be
or won't begin. The hours quickening,
never asleep. Or the trees' silence incanting
I'll never belong. My silent habit
is to listen:

                    for I knew these trees once
as a different self. I'll never speak
to her again or stand outside
like the trees, attending to what's
limitless, the sky, stray faces
at stray windows.

                  I couldn't hear back then,
walking the night forest, not trusting how
to follow. How to wend. Now it's the noise
of mastery, the mastery of being
alive—annoyed. I've said my piece
is what I'd like to say, or my peace

is still a part of there. I'm bad
at idiom, as anyone can hear,
as anyone can see, there's an
immigrant on my face,

                      who makes me stray,
makes me tired of you and you and you, all of you
the never outside my window. Here, I turn
to stone, turn to the body in the dark.
I turn mortal and loathsome as bitumen
blacking out a new roof. I turn
at Florida Avenue, up 16th. I turn like milk,
unforgivably sour. A sudden turncoat,
I'll turn on you. My ideology,
a tourniquet. I turn my face
towards your light, alas, the last of which
will not return to me. I'm turning
off now—

              Good night, America. Good night, neighbor.
I did not know your art was law, or that you sailed
a boat on the Potomac, could parse the grammar
of daffodils.... Tonight is Sunday; on Friday
you died. Crowding the mail room with you last week,
I wondered whether to note the winter
drag, the government shut down again
by brief-falling snow. Neighbor, I junked
circulars and lost hope. I sighed, let my son cry
too loudly, Bonnie, Bonnie rather than turn to you
to wish you good night, good night....

              Dear Bonnie, I wish you good night.

MODERNITY

when I think about the smallness of my life
    when I think about the time you didn't
        when I think about the need every day

to raze another building to raise another building hard
    hats walk steel beams outside my window they walk
        the sky where cranes rule concrete it reaches higher

every day when I think about where my sight meets them
    at their feet I'm on the sixth floor again when
        I think about the ordinary sight of construction

brick and mortar so many faceless men and women
    fill out the skeleton of a mid-rise mortality oh the epiphanic
        mundane oh what I build and cannot build

when I think about the hollow poems the hollowness
    at the heart of my heart I have changed
        have I changed how have I changed if

that is the ground and not the figure or if that
    is the figure and not the ground all men kill
        the thing they love Wilde wrote white streaks

on the green radiance like memory loosening
    from the trees a hollow of skin under each green eye
        must I remember eyeing you on 8th Ave

I've already forgotten yes I have forgotten
    the silence of that rooftop party in Chelsea
        I was talking to a man named Trenton saying

you're my state capital standing too close to him
            when I was looking not at NJ but you later I let you
                        walk me home the next day we saw tapestries

at the museum when I think about the unicorn
            in captivity the garden a symbol of the fence a
                      symbol of what is made a symbol of form I'm still

held by your voice so often in motion I rise to
            words suddenly taller than the park's stone walls
                      then a courtyard of marble cold echo of Sunday

morning the complacency of a cold godless thing
            we didn't want to leave the museum we didn't
                      want noon heat to assault us it's hard

to remember younger bodies younger
            more careless did you care that the tapestries
                      caught us in another crowd no longer

resplendent when once a world of so many hands
            wove wool warp with wool silk
                      silver and gilt welts wove the nameless

threads our mythology wrecked by daylight
            that first day of August summer perfected our
                      slow graceless paces when I think about

how often we wept for art the realm of
            our artlessness when I think about how sure our art
                      would fail the mess we made of art our selves

quando Amor mi spira… is nothing love nothing
            nothing did I know when I counted fruit
                      in the pomegranate tree the ornate chain

around the unicorn's neck barely buckled yet
      bound I did not see until recently the cradled
            hoofs the trial of humility red seeds promising

future bounty when I think about this age
      I'd never thought we'd be so old so gray or
            how even young we never chose to be free

EPISTEME 30

I did not know
your joy. I
found a recess

in my climb,
where
the oak lost

the tread for
its roots and fell. Falling,
too, I grew

out of dying
and that
desire we once

caught on another
mountain. If
we could pause, I

would write
of the blur I woke to
today, gold

light, a love
the gut of
a shadow can't

fathom. I am
only yours
if the world

were yours
to lose. This is a
game: name the leaf

that won't color,
the char
of sleep, what's burnt

isn't gone. I am here.
I am here. There
is no you.

DOROTHY
WORDSWORTH

The daffodils can go fuck themselves.
I'm tired of their crowds, yellow rantings
about the spastic sun that shines and shines
and shines. How are they any different

from me? I, too, have a big messy head
on a fragile stalk. I spin with the wind.
I flower and don't apologize. There's nothing
funny about good weather. Oh, spring again,

the critics nod. They know the old joy,
that wakeful quotidian, the dark plot
of future growing things, each one
labeled *Narcissus nobilis* or *Jennifer Chang*.

If I died falling from a helicopter, then
this would be an important poem. Then
the ex-boyfriends would swim to shore
declaiming their knowledge of my bulbous

youth. O, Flower, one said, why aren't you
meat? But I won't be another bashful shank.
The tulips have their nervous *joie de vivre*,
the lilacs their taunt. Fractious petals, stop

interrupting me with your boring beauty.
All the boys are in the field gnawing raw
bones of ambition and calling it ardor. Who
the hell are they? This is a poem about war.

LET'S NAME OUR SON
AFTER FRANK O'HARA

as another dead poet passes by

the boy is growing every day

Le Balcon or *Les Nègres* of Genet

every day a dream of words

like darts chasing the bull's-eye

then I wake up and I'm married

to the floor my body a sorry shaft

the other side of what I mean

every day the boy eats the fruit

of screaming once I saw

a Dutch painter after waiting

in line for two hours he was

older than Manhattan what

was his name he drew the light

it was winter the Frick look

gray lucent fields an unadorned

profile plain as the sun and now

maybe the boy is dying or another

word for not quite living is waiting

inside of me there should be

so much more it is March it is April

garbage trucks percuss the spring

is it not wisdom to explain hello

cold pussy willow solemn Ohio

get out from behind the tree you

are not an orphan stop crying

you echo of a poem I am guilty

and the sky is blue the sky is blue

AGAIN A SOLSTICE

It is not good to think
of everything as a mistake. I asked
for bacon in my sandwich, and then

I asked for more. Mistake.
I told you the truth about my scar:

I did not use a knife. I lied
about what he did to my faith
in loneliness. Both mistakes.

That there is always a you. Mistake.
Faith in loneliness, my mother proclaimed,

is faith in self. My instinct, a poor Polaris.
Not a mistake is the blue boredom
of a summer lake. O mud, sun, and algae!

We swim in glittering murk.
I tread, you tread. There are children

testing the deep end, shriek and stroke,
the lifeguard perilously close to diving.
I tried diving once. I dove like a brick.

It was a mistake to ask the $30 prophet
for a $20 prophecy. A mistake to believe.

I was young and broke. I swam
in a stolen reservoir then, not even a lake.
Her prophesy: from my vagrant exertion

I'll die at 42. Our dog totters across the lake,
kicks the ripple. I tread, you tread.

What does it even mean to write a poem?
It means today
I'm correcting my mistakes.

It means I don't want to be lonely.

WE FOUND THE BODY
OF A YOUNG DEER ONCE

Whitetails flicker like light in the winter woods,
where my dog and I crack open
the early morning, the ground a frozen patchwork
of leaves, the brittle ice of dirt. So much
of walking is description. Late in the year
the sun stops us cold. Or, walking is comparison,
these woods in New Jersey seem
                    (a passing thought) Ohioan,
                    then I recall that late thaw
one March in New Hampshire. Or,
                            I'm ten again wondering where
                            I last saw the deer carcass. Maybe

by the creek, maybe loose ribs, a skull
tucked into snow.
                    As children
we set old logs against a middling elm,
thatched branches
into a sort of rooftop, called our dwelling
Antelope. My friend and I, we ignored the sky
cutting into our shelter and made walls
of found particleboard,
                    fragmentary, damp, worthless as kindling.
                    Her mother worshipped Zoroaster. Her father
had an Irish-American mistress. Stub of birch, first rime
graying the last moss,
the ground fascinates a spray
of blue jays.
            Because the earth won't hold
                    together, deeper in
        is still nowhere. I've dug through seasons of leaves,

cold rot, hardly insoluble, crumbling
through my fingers.
              I climbed a tree,
crossed a swamp in bare feet. I judged
the clouds for their blue avarice,
foolish dispersal.
            At home she spoke her language, and I at mine.
Where do the frogs go in winter?
What time is it? I hated her for being braver.

She wanted habits to make sense.
She liked to win. Every day she needed to know
where I was going.
             But the best walking is without
reason, formless, scattering the self
into thinking, more winter. The deer were fleet, mild,

and unassuming.
I want to describe them
              as darts, though they evinced no danger—
              legs limber, outflung,
              almost tree-like in their slender extension,
almost flying.
In their swift silence, an anxiety.
              They flee from me; they fled.
              I had made a noise,
              my dog's breath quickening, my interest
remapping the woods as suddenly more
mine.
            An image I know well,
yet nevertheless
despise. Is the past a failure, or am I?
                    Whose woods these are, after all,
is a question only a god would ask:
              so, yes, my sight seizes all, a memory of
land, a friend I'll never see again.

Her father, as a university student, had dined with the Shah.
Whenever her mother polished the silver we'd joke,
The Shah is coming to tea!
                              From upstairs
                              we could smell duck stewing in walnuts
and pomegranate syrup. Later, the darkest meat
fell to pieces onto bright, particulate rice.

It was like eating a secret, my mouth
stunned by acid sweetness, a terrible hunger
I could not explain to my own mother.
I wanted more, another plate of *fesenjan*, please—

instead: into the winter woods we ran
after this new world
that knew nothing of what we hid
on our tongues—other words for dusk,
revolution, and snow.
                    We dismissed our appetites. We forgot our fathers.

I love the birches
                    for their austerity: the peeling white bark,
                    pages torn from an old book. I love

the outstretched affirmation of oaks,
more certain in leaflessness. In winter

                              you have to know the bark to know the tree,
                              you have to look hard and not doubt
                              the spine and bole. Branches, twigs, roots

often foster anonymity, and this, too,
I love.
            Farther, farther, I am going into the dark

of the mind, that neighbor girl, my friend—she goes
by Mrs. Black now, so I hear, lives out west,

plants tulips every November, and, come spring,
scythes each one mid-stem.
A crystal vase in the breakfast nook.
Cheerios in her sons' bowls, her dumb accomplished husband nodding
at the clock.

      It was with her I found
      the body of a young deer, fallen in a clearing,

fresh snow
powdering the deer's coat like ash
fallen from a proximate fire.

      Quiet,
          quieter than I've ever been
with anyone, we shared the death, we stood quietly, the sky

open and gray above us.
We never said a word about the deer. I imagine that winter
as helming decay, the woods

beastly, skeletal, far reach of the trees,
the deer's bone-cage
stripped clean of flesh.

      She showed me a map of Iran
      in my father's *World Atlas*. In Tehran, they had had
      many servants, including a gardener and a
night nurse for her and her brother,
though she was too young
to remember any of this.

      The day after solstice I note
an emerald shine to the pale sky.

      On the question of origin, she explained, *Persian*.
        Once I described my mother as always angry
(she was born amid a civil war), but mostly

my childhood was a quiet one. It was not
until years later that I learned
others had considered our family strange.

THE WORLD

One winter I lived north, alone
and effortless, dreaming myself
into the past. Perhaps, I thought,
words could replenish privacy.
Outside, a red bicycle froze
into form, made the world falser
in its white austerity. So much
happens after harvest: the moon
performing novelty: slaughter,
snow. One hour the same
as the next, I held my own hands
or held the snow. I was like sculpture,
forgetting or, perhaps, remembering
everything. Red wings in the snow,
red thoughts ablaze in the war
I was having with myself again.
Everything I hate about the world
I hate about myself, even now
writing as if this were a law
of nature. Say there were deer
fleet in the snow, walking out
the cold, and more gingkoes
bare in the beggar's grove. Say
I was not the only one who saw
or heard the trees, their diffidence
greater than my noise. Perhaps
the future is a tiny flame
I'll nick from a candle. First, I'm burning.
Then, numb. Why must every winter
grow colder, and more sure?

FUTURE SNOW

On the phone, my mother describes a show in which two people live on a stage in front of an audience. The audience goes home at night, but the two people stay on the stage, sleeping on their stage bed, waking to their stage breakfast nook.

At night, they exist in the dull light of exit signs. But these exits are not for the two people on the stage, where they now live wedded to calamity. Where they must stay for an unknown number of days. I ask my mother if she watches the audience or the two people on the stage. She does not think this is the right question.

The two people on the stage are as bored as she is, only she has no audience other than her children. I call her on the weekend to ask about her week; she tells me about a television show. Are the two people married? Do they have a window? Are we the children of an idle brain? Again, these are not the right questions.

When I watch two people on stage, I indulge in the belief that everyone is listening. Every word that is spoken makes the speaker more real. Soon she pierces the fearful hollow of my ear, and I am only listening to her. She is misreading the world. She will do this until the world is corrected, or she is. *It is night*, she insists. A noise from outside tells her so, a meteor exhaling. He disagrees, but what does it matter?

I know it is night. I hear a stranger pacing the sidewalk outside our house, which reminds me to lock the front door. Our house shall have no plague. There are those in the audience who will stay through the night because they believe what he says, *Night is over, and day is coming.* I would say they are all mistaken, even she is mistaken, but I am no longer listening.

Our streetlamp flickered out two nights ago. We are expecting an evening snow.

LOST CHILD

It is possible I've written all I can
about her, my friend, who once saw
my coldness, young as we were, as
might. Wordless, slow,

I watched her reach the green apex,
our forest unfolding a bolder spring,
then nodded at her victory. She won
the race. I did not

care: poor at math, wasteful of time—
those lush arrogant clouds—, I grazed
lawns, wrote poems. It is possible
ours was a friendship

of convenience. Neighbors, two
daughters of immigrants, we found
each other circling cul-de-sacs, an
afternoon's easy

drag, our bicycle wheels dulled by idle
lulling. What do I care now that she's
dying or about to die? Dark-haired, grave-
eyed, she was almost

beautiful. *What's a fish without an eye?*
FSHHH! A joke she'd tell past eighteen,
as if joking were the joke. Words to her
an affect of breath,

distractions apportioning the hour's
tedious orbit. I don't remember
laughing, or I did laugh because
I did love her

for giving me time to breathe,
to be and feel all that I was not
feeling—you know, that suburban
psychosis: *sad.*

I was a child so lost I froze
whenever she wept, posing like
preadolescent topiary, tireless,
another dud hedge

stalling on the lawn. Worse, I'd tell
the joke back to her—*What's a
fish?*—forgetting the crucial ocular,
the self. My closet

hid a packed bag. I swore I'd run away,
then didn't. I'd avoid phone calls, fib
my RSVP. *I was busy, am busy, will always
be busy!* Perhaps

this mirror can be comfort now, my face
vacant, wondering who she is to me,
more time wasted on the unknowable
sky, which is just

an image of the future. Fear lights
my eyes, and I blink, a self-enforced
detachment that self-soothes. I was
lonely, had no one

to sit on the bus or eat lunch with,
and even then knew I'd fail at
the most basic things. D+ in Human
Physiology, a first

marriage I didn't intend, ordinary
confessions pouring out as soon as
my lips kissed a cold rim of gin:
I stole my sister's

gold woolen capelet, I never loved
him. The truth is I learned nothing
from her kindness, and so confessing
now is folly, when

aging imposes new precision. Our
sons grow tall, our thoughts bleaker.
If the diagnosis surprised her, I'll
never know, and that

might be the end of it, if any end
could be tolerable. Imaginable.
I have no right to this poem, this life
insufficient

with gratitude, the unceasing toll
of tides outside my mind's window.
I have no right to see an end.
Outside the real

window a neighbor I've never spoken to
frees brambles of branches
knotted since winter from a rose shrub.
Though all's fruitless,

unsung, the thaw began last week
and I can say with certainty today
it is spring. I cannot say what I'd say
to her today

if she rose out of bed, head shorn,
bone-stemmed, and acknowledged me.
Would acknowledgment be her
immensity or

mine? It's work to gather the seasons,
to ask a question that finds the feeling
at the troubled core of thought. Tonight
I feel small and

not immense. Spring is dark like winter,
dark like children who've all summer traced
miles of asphalt with bare feet, bare arms,
bare insolent sun.

Again, I haven't traveled far enough.
Spring is a stark garden, is rude and
weary, a sole crocus, is grass, raw
tonight, too soon done.

INSIDE VOICE

Everyone is screaming inside
is a thought I've held dear
my whole life. I picture holes
opening up inside and

outside myself, the mouth
of the earth opening, cloudless
holes in the sky, oh,
that I cannot scream, my head empties,

stomach gone, a sole lung vacating
the body, the gulf of me, newly
voided. A child has a small voice,
I tell my son, as our chorus teacher

told me decades ago, and it is not true.
He screams down every aisle of Petco:
zebra finch, parakeet, angelfish,
mollies. He's such a scream!

Parenting, such a scream! *Use your
inside voice*, I calmly advise, calmly
chasing him, calm as the books
advise, calm being we want

him to become, one of the
very calm citizenry. I sing my ditty
past buckets of litter clumping and dust-free—
Use it or lose it, as if his voice could

simply drop to the floor, as if I'd
snatch it from his throat. *Use it or lose it*,
one says of resources natural
and otherwise, my bargain with

the planet, this corner of Petco
where the words *Please don't
hit me* sputter out of a girl's mouth
to a man, her father or just a man, whose fists

perch on the ledge of his belt, hawk-like,
relentless; his voice swooping down
to her, a dangerous pitch. I can only hear
punctured consonants,

a voice inside and yet too far
outside. My eyes catch my son
by the cats, each king
to a plain plastic box. The calico

pacing a brief perimeter, the golden
tabby's muzzle learning my son's
invading paw.
Be gentle, I should say,

but my voice makes a poor cage.
There is the man and the girl. There is
the store clerk, a teenaged boy pushing a cart
of automatic feeders. There is the corn snake,

the dalmatian rat, the long-tailed lizard, past,
present, and future selves;
and yes, there are the cats,
unwanted, wanting

a sun spot all their own.
What we know as home
the cats will colonize, stretch their gaze
to stake territories, another

arbitrary boundary: what we know
as home is speculation, the other
person who may or may not
love you back depending on

the weather, whether the mortgage is paid,
the softness of today's boiled egg.
I want to scream.
I want the girl to scream.

Look away. The cats will not stop
the screaming inside
our heads. How do I protect them
from my son's rough reach? His voice

fills cages with bright
admonishing, accusing
the cats of what they can't help
but be: CAT

CAT CAT. I am the cat's,
the cat is mine,
his voice too loud
to not stand as authority. *Use it or lose it*,

I'm fuzzy on the antecedent now.
His voice, my
authority? The cats, the girl?
It is Sunday,

quarter to ten; in my bag, here's
inventory: the blankie, the house keys,
two stale knots of bread. Who am I
to call myself human?

THE STRANGERS

1

Mostly, I hope.

2

In the industry of specifics, I list my Sally-trees, my letters to Paul.

3

Everyone is speaking at the same time; the rain is speaking at the same time.

4

Strangers stand in the avenues, in the meadowlands, in the waiting rooms of mightier offices.

5

They are looking at their hands, thinking they are looking at the past.

6

This is the ordinary march to justice, Mary Wollstonecraft writes.

7

Reader, they are looking at the future.

8

Look:

9

I have the hands of an American poet.

10

Sally wields her radiant leaves, while Paul is sincerely, always, yours sincerely.

11

What if? I ask the strangers.

12

Mostly, I hope for snow in winter and the fortitude to bear it.

13

I ask the strangers, *If love were privation, and therefore infinitely imaginable, would I nurse such rootless sentiments?*

14

Would I hope myself into yet another quiet vessel, striving against bad weather?

15

This vessel, an argument against vindication.

16

I am not sure why the strangers have made a home of everywhere, why the veins of their palms whorl in the wrong direction, but I reach out to them.

17

Our very soul expands, and we forget our littleness, Mary Wollstonecraft writes.

18

West, west, all the strangers are heading west into the prairies and then the mountains and then the coastal cities, like a flock of water-hungry lemmings, like a flock without fear.

19

And if there is no future snow, then will there be neither catastrophe nor love?

20

Mostly, I hope to write back Paul.

21

When the strangers reach ocean they see they have not in fact reached home, their hands, white flags hailing the furious shore.

22

Or: the wave-stressed shore, the shore queening its pale strand over the world's erosion.

23

Dear Paul, When you died, I knew that love held a terminus too dear, and it is strange to love what won't be, and to be every dead thing is stranger.

24

Dear Paul, I miss chiming in the dark.

25

Mostly, I hope to fill the blank pages of your hands with snow and doubt.

26

But to return to the straight road of observation, Mary Wollstonecraft writes.

27

If love is not privation, then is it too much, is it too much, it is much too much.

28

And now I explain to Sally that the remnant prairie is also not love, however long it frets.

29

It is not yet winter.

30

I have been awake in your silence.

31

The strangers grow tired of poetry and will not sit in the light.

CEREMONY

I can't say which
cloud cut open
the hill. Or why,
walking, I can't
reach the sky. Virginia
is not east.
          The hill
gives no slack, no
shade, so I rise
to light. I am quiet
and won't
squander words
to make what's
false true.
          I had
a love. A blue
kite untwisting
the sky.

SIGNS

Stranger, don't refuse me, vagabond that I am—
I beg you, tell me what I need to know.
— Oedipus at Colonus

The light above us,
my son decides, is an erratic bird.
Index finger to thumb, he makes the sign,
a sudden beak in his tiny, tensed hand.
All he knows is animal, noun. An elephant looms
from a zoo poster and his arm is now
a flagrant trunk in the Metro car, swinging away,
swinging up to his stroller's black canopy.
Our train shudders past Farragut West
to McPherson Square, an electric surge,
weird blinking that takes us in and out
of darkness, and in this pause of light
a man and his daughter guide themselves
into our car. They collapse

their white canes, embrace the pole.
Tall and blind, they usher their faces
close in conversation no one can hear, though
there is always a way to imagine
what a daughter says to her father
to make him smile and shake his head.
She has his chin, a soft bulb of flesh, a softer
jaw. The mind's clock is unwinding
thought by thought. Little clicks. Windows bleak
with soot don't tell time, yet every face my son spies

is sharpened by boredom. Thus, the boredom
of a blind father and blind daughter
shames my curiosity. I am looking too hard
at my son looking at the crowd
we sit in. Station to station, we stop and go, open
and shut, we meet the windows'
blank stares. Little clicks, darkening
speed: one day I'll have to explain
prepositions, the extravagance of adverbs,
le mot juste. This is the safest route

to the closest Metro stop. Here is the library, here
the public park. Wait your turn on the slide.
Say *Excuse me. Gesundheit.* Please.
It is hard to live in the city.

Do not stand on the platform's granite edge
is one warning. The meanness of the future, another:
how it thrusts our boredom forward to where
we all disappear. It means so little,
our means so scarce. At Eastern Market
I push his stroller out of the car
and cannot see what signs he gives
the father and daughter, who began
ahead of us. Their white canes, deliberate,
direct, tap out the traffic of too many
voices in, I imagine, I don't know why,
4/4 time. Every stranger is a child of hurry
and remorse, but it's this one I follow,
my son. We named him after a wanderer.

ABOUT TREES

What I would say about certain trees

is that to master love one must be devastated by it.
Certain trees know.

A poem has nothing to do with fact,
though both are made things.
I explain that certain trees know
certain facts, but what poems.

Our son is a rutabaga.
To him, everything
is a rutabaga.

———

What were we talking about last night,
listening to the fan, falling asleep?

———

I've been thinking about things
as the source from which all thought rises.
Not as omens, signs, talismans, tokens, symbols,
figures of speech, or ideas.

A thing introduces a thought and is never more than a thing.
Yes, that sounds right.

The E detached from my silver love ring;

there was no meaning to it, though now I know
the saleswoman was likely false. Her calming nod

against fragility. It will tarnish,
but it will not crack
as the plates will crack. The thought

of you not listening when I ask again
what it means.

Family heirloom plates I hate. These small windows
bring in no light.

I've stared at what's most broken in you.

An unintelligibility

to the flat sheet sliding off of me,
a silent body is not always asleep.

Even when happiest I think about dying.

——

I want to remember how

his face turned down

and took away our light

to become a first order of love.

———

A woman once opened my hand in her smoked palms
and told me I would be dead in a week.

Then put out your cigarette right here,
I dared, pointing to
my truth spot

or whatever she called it,
a whisper of a wrinkle on my skin.

That's the story you'd like me to tell
as our son naps fitfully in the other room.
Also the one about swimming

on a high floor of the Hancock Tower.
Both stories end the same way.

———

Crust of sugar at the bottom of your glass.
Keys to whatever doors we've forgotten.
Mostly used lipstick in Shanghai Nights,
a garish red. The paper sheath of a straw
which for a precious five minutes served as his toy.
Little notes to myself I can't bear to throw away.
All waste we shall bequeath to our heir.   Our air.

———

Envoi

Trees older than your father and me
line the trail on which we lose ourselves.
I think they are maples. Their leaves wave to us,

a rapt audience to our stolen afternoon.
I think you said father before mother
in Chinese, *Bà ba*,

already I cannot remember.

The hills are older, too, and may outlive you.

The sky is eternity, but the clouds are brief.

New logs cleared from last week's storm,
their moisture forms new fungus,
new sights for you, the things that make

whatever words I choose stranger
and more true. Often

I'm struck dumb by knowing
that until recently you did not exist,

the way I know one day I won't exist,
and that's a kind of prayer

I don't have the words for. Your father
and I are atheists, but you are free

to measure the sky as you will and decide
accordingly. I never thought there'd be a you:
fact or poem, you're child to a thought
we once had.

I remember standing

in the cemetery with your father,
his long black coat, a woolen harbor

against that relentless winter,
wondering why love is harder
than speech. When we were so quiet.

The wind knew before we knew, and then the wind was gone.

NOTES

The book's title is from *Romeo and Juliet*. In Act III, Scene V, Juliet admits to willfully misinterpreting the birdsong they hear as nightingales in order to claim it is night and keep Romeo by her side. She reasons:

> Some say the lark makes sweet division;
> This doth not so, for she divideth us.
> Some say the lark and loathèd toad change eyes;
> O, now I would they had changed voices too,
> Since arm from arm that voice doth us affray

"A Horse Named Never"
Among the horses Thomas Jefferson kept at his Virginia home Monticello were Biscuit and Crab, but there was no horse named Never, nor a Trapezoid. The first italicized line is from W. B. Yeats's essay "Emotion on Multitude," though I've replaced "Lear" in the sentence with "horse." The second italicized line is from Richard III, though I've replaced "Richmonds" with "horses."

"The Winter's Wife"
The title is from Wallace Stevens's "Vita Mea," a poem composed in 1898. The nineteen-year-old Stevens wrote:

> And what sweet wind was rife
> With earth, or sea, or star, or new sun's bloom,
> Lay sick and dead within that place of doom,
> Where I went raving like the winter's wife.
> "In vain, In vain," with bitter lips I cried

"There Are Too Many Other Birds to Write About"
The grave of Edith Lewis is located in Jaffrey, New Hampshire beside the grave of her lifelong partner, Willa Cather.

"The River Pilgrims"
The missing body depicted and sought out in "River Pilgrims" pays
homage to the missing body of Robert Nguyen, a thirty-year-old New
Jersey police officer, who accidently drove off of Lincoln Highway Bridge
on the evening of December 25, 2005. The dense fog that night made
it impossible to see that the bridge was lifted, awaiting passage of a
boat. While the body of his partner, Shawn Carson, was quickly found,
searchers combed the Hackensack River for four days before finally
recovering Nguyen's body.

"Freedom in Ohio"
On October 18, 2011, a man in Zanesville, Ohio released several
dozen wild animals he'd kept in captivity on a private reserve before
committing suicide. The animals roamed fields and nearby highways
freely until law enforcement officials shot and killed forty-nine of them,
including eighteen Bengal tigers.

"Myself—be Noon to Him"
The title is from Emily Dickinson's Poem 368 in R. W. Franklin's
edition::

> I envy Light – that wakes Him –
> And Bells – that boldly ring
> To tell Him it is Noon, abroad –
> Myself – be Noon to Him –
>
> Yet interdict – my Blossom –
> And abrogate – my Bee –
> Lest Noon in everlasting night –
> Drop Gabriel – and me –

"Habit"
The poem is inspired, in part, by the journals of Dorothy Wordsworth
and, in part, by a years-long conversation with Cecily Parks, who
introduced me to these journals. The poem is for her and Miss
Wordsworth.

"Episteme 12"
The last lines are from Susan Fenimore Cooper's *Rural Hours, a nature diary of Cooperstown, NY* (1850).

"Mount Pleasant"
The poem is modeled after Samuel Taylor Coleridge's "Frost at Midnight."

"Modernity"
The poem borrows a line from Canto XXIV of Dante's *Purgatorio*, which reads in its entirety: "I' mi son un che: quando Amor mi spira, noto," which translates as "I am one who, when loves breathes in me, takes note." I'm grateful to Katherine Wasdin for helping me understand the syntax and various translations of the Italian.

"Let's Name Our Son after Frank O'Hara"
The poem takes language from the following Frank O'Hara poems: "The Day Lady Died," "Why I Am Not a Painter," "For Grace after a Party," and "Autobiographia Literaria."

"Again a Solstice"
The title is from Thomas Browne's *Religio Medici* (1643) and appears in a lyric interlude within the prose:

> So when thy absent Beams begin t'impart
> Again a Solstice on my frozen Heart,
> My Winter's o'er, my drooping Spirits sing
> And ev'ry Part revives into a Spring.

"Future Snow"
The poem takes language from *Romeo and Juliet*.

"The Strangers"
The quotations from Mary Wollstonecraft are from *Letters Written during a Short Residence in Sweden, Norway, and Denmark* (1796), which was published four years after *Vindication for the Rights of Women*. Crafted from letters and journal entries, this odd book recounts three

months when Wollstonecraft tried to recover a treasure ship belonging to her estranged lover, though the narrative includes no mention of him or their relationship, focusing instead on her observations on Scandinavian life and culture and traveling as a solitary woman. The phrase "every dead thing" is from John Donne's "A Nocturnal upon St. Lucy's Day." "The Strangers" is for Sally Wen Mao and Paul Legault, who are real-life poets but not real-life people.

RECENT TITLES FROM
ALICE JAMES BOOKS

Calling a Wolf a Wolf, Kaveh Akbar
We're On: A June Jordan Reader, Edited by Christoph Keller and Jan Heller Levi
Daylily Called It a Dangerous Moment, Alessandra Lynch
Surgical Wing, Kristin Robertson
The Blessing of Dark Water, Elizabeth Lyons
Reaper, Jill McDonough
Madwoman, Shara McCallum
Contradictions in the Design, Matthew Olzmann
House of Water, Matthew Nienow
World of Made and Unmade, Jane Mead
Driving without a License, Janine Joseph
The Big Book of Exit Strategies, Jamaal May
play dead, francine j. harris
Thief in the Interior, Phillip B. Williams
Second Empire, Richie Hofmann
Drought-Adapted Vine, Donald Revell
Refuge/es, Michael Broek
O'Nights, Cecily Parks
Yearling, Lo Kwa Mei-en
Sand Opera, Philip Metres
Devil, Dear, Mary Ann McFadden
Eros Is More, Juan Antonio González Iglesias, Translated by Curtis Bauer
Mad Honey Symposium, Sally Wen Mao
Split, Cathy Linh Che
Money Money Money | Water Water Water, Jane Mead
Orphan, Jan Heller Levi
Hum, Jamaal May
Viral, Suzanne Parker
We Come Elemental, Tamiko Beyer
Obscenely Yours, Angelo Nikolopoulos

Alice James Books has been publishing poetry since 1973. The press was founded in Boston, Massachusetts as a cooperative wherein authors performed the day-to-day undertakings of the press. This collaborative element remains viable even today, as authors who publish with the press are also invited to become members of the editorial board and participate in editorial decisions at the press. The editorial board selects manuscripts for publication via the press's annual, national competition, the Alice James Award. Alice James Books seeks to support women writers and was named for Alice James, sister to William and Henry, whose extraordinary gift for writing went unrecognized during her lifetime.

Printed by McNaughton & Gunn